WHAT'S THE WEATHER?

IT'S SUNNY

Written by
William Anthony

KidHaven PUBLISHING

Published in 2023 by **KidHaven Publishing, an Imprint of Greenhaven Publishing, LLC**
29 East 21st Street
New York, NY 10010

Edited by: Shalini Vallepur

Designed by: Danielle Webster-Jones

Cataloging-in-Publication Data

Names: Anthony, William, 1996-.
Title: It's sunny / William Anthony.
Description: New York : KidHaven Publishing, 2023. | Series: What's the weather? | Includes glossary and index.
Identifiers: ISBN 9781534540736 (pbk.) |
ISBN 9781534540750 (library bound) |
ISBN 9781534540743 (6 pack) |
ISBN 9781534540767 (ebook)
Subjects: LCSH: Sunshine--Juvenile literature. | Weather--Juvenile literature. | Sun--Juvenile literature.
Classification: LCC QC911.2 A58 2023 |
DDC 551.5'271--dc23

Manufactured in the United States of America

CPSIA compliance information: Batch #CSKH23: For further information contact Greenhaven Publishing LLC, New York, New York at 1-844-317-7404.

Please visit our website, www.greenhavenpublishing.com. For a free color catalog of all our high-quality books, call toll free 1-844-317-7404 or fax 1-844-317-7405.

Find us on

PHOTO CREDITS

All images are courtesy of Shutterstock.com, unless otherwise specified. With thanks to Getty Images, Thinkstock Photo and iStockphoto. Front Cover – MarKord, Subbotina Anna, Big Foot Productions, maxim ibragimov, SunKids. Character throughout – yusufdemirci. 4 – Fancy Tapis, Dark Moon Pictures, Iryna Alex, Tiina Tuomaala. 5 – Kichigin. 6 – Incomible. 7 – Africa Studio 8 – Africa Studio. 9 – AlinaMD. 10 – Amanda Carden. 11 – imtmphoto. 12 – wavebreakmedia. 13 – yusufdemirci, Elena Efimova. 14 – Sergey Novikov. 15 – BIGANDT.COM. 16 – werber photography. 17 – Sunny studio. 18 – DRidgway. 19 – anetapics. 20–21 – Bumble Dee. 22 – wk1003mike. 23 – Luca Santilli.

CONTENTS

Page 4 What Can You See?
Page 6 Seasons
Page 8 It's Sunny!
Page 10 The Sun
Page 12 What to Wear
Page 14 Fun in the Sun
Page 16 Plants
Page 18 Animals
Page 20 Wildfires
Page 22 Safe in the Sun
Page 24 Glossary and Index

WHAT CAN YOU SEE?

Take a peek out of the window. What can you see? Are the trees blowing around or are they covered in something powdery and white?

Weather is what you can see in the sky and feel in the air outside. There are many types of weather, such as sunshine, snow, wind, and rain.

SEASONS

In many places, there are four seasons every year. They are spring, summer, autumn, and winter. Different types of weather may happen in each season.

Summer is the warmest season. In summer, you may see lots of sunshine, but you probably won't see any snow.

IT'S SUNNY!

We say it is sunny when we can see the sun in the sky and nothing is blocking it out. The world around you will look bright and colorful.

When it's sunny, you may not see many clouds in the sky. The sky may be bright and blue.

THE SUN

Earth and seven other planets all move around the sun in space.

We get sunshine from the sun. The sun is a big ball of burning gas. It is a very long way from Earth.

We get all of our natural light from the sun. This helps us see during the daytime. The sun also gives us heat, which helps keep us warm.

WHAT TO WEAR

During the summer, sunny days may get quite warm. It's good to wear loose-fitting clothes such as T-shirts, skirts, and shorts. These will help you to keep cool.

In winter, sunny days can be cold. Don't forget to dress warmly!

If you are out in the sunshine for a long time, it is a good idea to wear a hat and sunglasses. These will protect your head and your eyes.

Never look straight at the sun, even with sunglasses on.

FUN IN THE SUN

Sunny weather is perfect for having fun outside. Many people travel to the beach for a fun day out in the sunshine.

When it's hot and sunny, you can swim to cool off. You can play water polo or have a swimming race.

PLANTS

Plants are living things. They need a few things to keep them alive, such as sunshine and warmth. Sunlight helps plants make the food they need in order to grow.

In spring and summer, there are many long, sunny days. In those seasons, you can see lots of flowers and trees starting to blossom.

ANIMALS

Many animals depend on plants for food. Sunshine helps plants grow. This means there will be more food for animals to eat.

This bear is eating berries.

Some animals are adapted to live in sunny weather. Meerkats have dark patches around their eyes that act like sunglasses.

WILDFIRES

Sometimes, the sun can cause damage. When an area such as a forest becomes very dry, a hot, sunny day might start a fire. This is called a wildfire.

Wildfires can destroy animal habitats. This means that many animals can lose their homes in a wildfire. Some wildfires can take a long time to be put out.

SAFE IN THE SUN

When you are out in the sunshine, it is important to protect yourself. Staying in the sun for too long can cause your skin to burn.

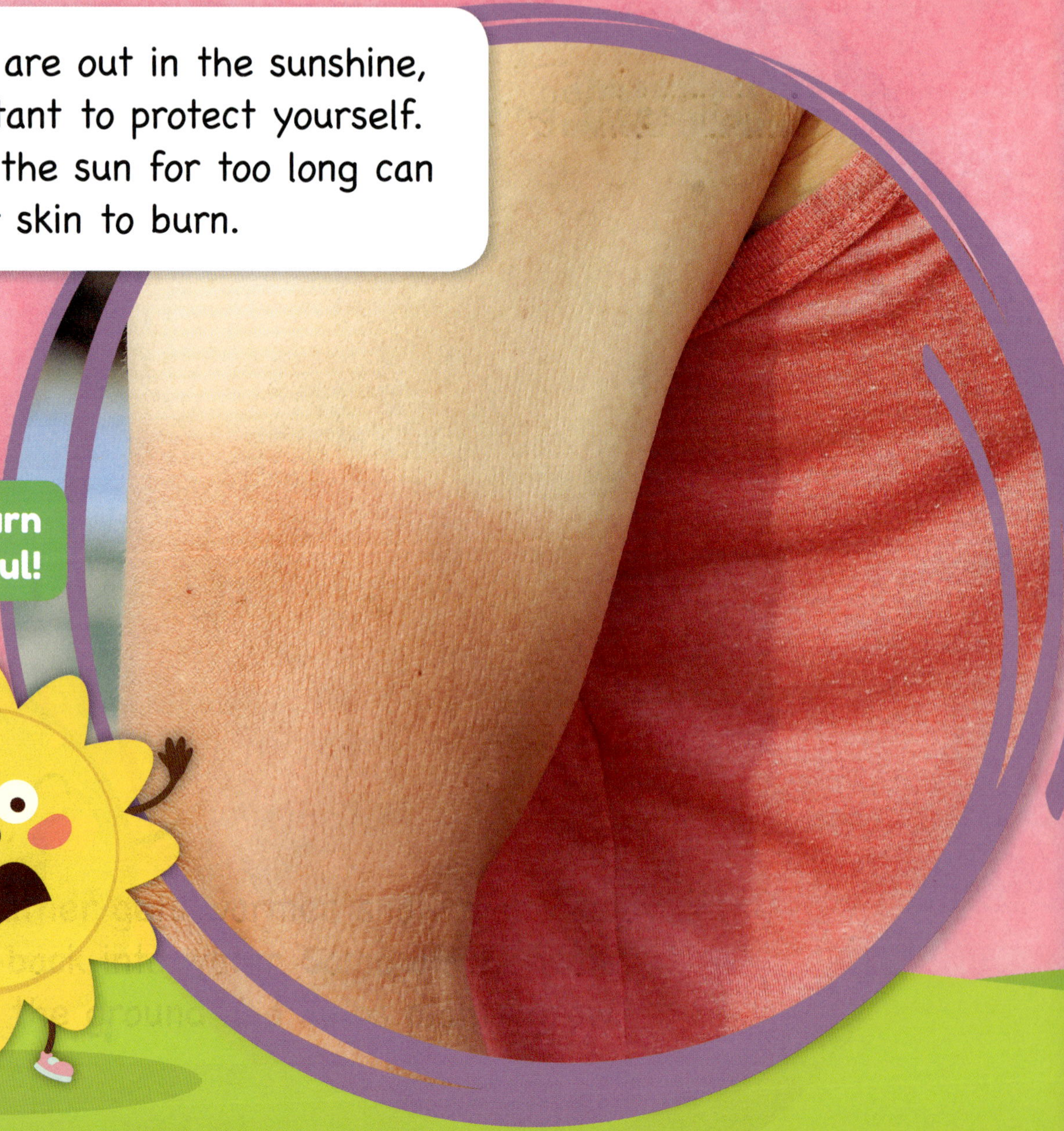

Sunscreen will help keep your skin from burning. A hat will keep your face in the shade. Sunglasses will protect your eyes from the bright light.

GLOSSARY

adapted	changed over time to suit the environment
blossom	to produce flowers
damage	harm that is done to something or someone
depend	to rely upon or need something
gas	a thing that is like air, which spreads out to fill any space available
habitats	the natural homes in which animals, plants, and other living things live
natural	found in nature and not made by people
planets	large, round objects in space (such as Earth) that travel around a star (such as the sun)
protect	to stop something from being harmed
water polo	a game played in water by two teams that try to score by throwing a ball into a goal

INDEX

animals 18–19, 21
beaches 14
clothes 12–13, 23
clouds 9
plants 16–18
seasons 6–7, 12, 17
sky 5, 8–9
sun 5, 8, 10–11, 13, 20
sunburn 22
sunscreen 23
sunshine 5, 7–10, 12–20, 22
swimming 15